Care
to
Communicate

Helping the Older Person with Dementia

Jennie Powell

Cardiff Memory Team
University Department of Geriatric Medicine
Llandough Hospital
Cardiff

Illustrations by Eve Morris

Journal of Dementia Care

A PRACTICAL GUIDE FOR CAREWORKERS

Acknowledgements
*Many of the ideas in this book have evolved
over time spent working with patients and colleagues of the
Cardiff Memory Team*

CARE TO COMMUNICATE

Helping the Older Person with Dementia

A PRACTICAL GUIDE FOR CAREWORKERS

First published in 2000, second edition 2007, reprinted 2012
Hawker Publications Ltd
Culvert House, Culvert Road
London SW11 5DH
Tel 020 7720 2108, fax 020 7498 3023
www.careinfo.org

British Library Cataloguing in Publication Data

A Catalogue in Publication Data

ISBN 9781874 790488

Designed by Jay Dowle and Sue Lishman

Printed and bound by DG3, London

Hawker Publications publishes *The Journal of Dementia Care.* For further information
please contact Hawker Publications at the address above, or see www.careinfo.org

Also published by Hawker Publications:

Designing homes for people with dementia By Damian Utton (2007 ISBN 9781874 790280)

Dementia: Walking not wandering Edited by Mary Marshall and Kate Allan (2006 ISBN 9781874 790686)

Food, glorious food – Perspectives on food and dementia. Edited by Mary Marshall (2000 ISBN 9781874 790716)

And Still The Music Plays – Stories of People with Dementia By Graham Stokes (2008 ISBN 9781874 790952)

Making a difference – An evidence-based group programme to offer cognitive stimulation therapy (CST) to people with dementia By Aimee Spector, Lene Thorgrimsen, Bob Woods and Martin Orrell (2006 ISBN 9781874 790785)

Making a Difference 2 – An evidence-based group programme to offer cognitive stimulation therapy (CST) to people with dementia. The manual for group leaders, vol 2 By Elisa Aguirre, Aimée Spector, Amy Streater, Juanita Hoe, Bob Woods and Martin Orrell (2012 ISBN 9781874 790990)

Chocolate Rain – 100 ideas for a creative approach to activities in dementia care By Sarah Zoutewelle-Morris (2011 ISBN 9781874 790969)

Dementia and Sexuality By Elaine White (2011 ISBN 9781874 790976)

Contents

**CLIPPER
Supplements**

Stage 1
Questionnaire

Stage 2
Worksheet

Stage 3
Clipper Plan

Stage 4
Clipper Review

Introduction

Dementia is the name given to a set of symptoms caused by an illness or disease that affects the brain. The symptoms include problems with memory, reasoning and judgement. The person therefore has difficulty thinking. The problems with thinking can lead to difficulties with communication, difficulty with managing day-to-day affairs, difficulty with self care, changes in behaviour and apparent changes in personality.

The most common type of dementia is Alzheimer's disease. Other dementias include vascular dementias such as multi-infarct dementia ("mini-strokes"), dementia with Lewy bodies, Pick's disease (frontal lobe dementia), Huntington's disease and dementia associated with Parkinson's disease. All these dementias are progressive so that over a period of time the symptoms will gradually worsen.

No two people with dementia are ever the same. Different parts of the brain may be affected or the brain may be affected in different ways. Also, some people with dementia are mildly impaired while others are at a later stage of the illness and have more severe problems. Beyond the disease itself is the individual who will respond to the illness in his or her own individual way.

Caring for people with dementia can be difficult. Problems with communication can be particularly stressful. Developing a good understanding of how and why communication may be affected can help people with dementia and their carers attain a higher quality of life.

The aims of this book are:

• To give an understanding of the normal communication process and how this may break down for elderly people

• To consider how communication may be affected in dementia

• To offer ideas that will help keep open good channels of communication, thereby encouraging the best possible quality of life.

Jennie A Powell PhD MSc MCSLT
Memory Team
University Department of Geriatric Medicine
Llandough Hospital
Cardiff CF64 2XX

Acknowledgements
Many of the ideas in this book have evolved over time spent working with patients and colleagues of the Memory Team, Llandough Hospital, Cardiff.

1 The normal communication process

• What is an idea? • Communicating ideas with words • Communicating ideas non-verbally: facial expression; eye contact; body language, gesture and touch; emotional tone of voice

People communicate with one another to express their needs, feelings and opinions or purely for enjoyment. Successful communication is when an idea is passed correctly from one person to another.

WHAT IS AN IDEA?

An idea may be thought of as a collection of images in the brain. The images are created out of memories (stored in the brain) of things we have experienced as we go through life.

For example, when asked to think of their idea of an apple, most people would conjure up images from memories of having had contact with an apple in the past. Visual or picture images are particularly important. The shape of the apple can be "seen" in your head, as can its colour, the dent in the top, the stalk, the sheen as it catches the light. The apple can be imagined in many different visual environments – on a tree, in an orchard, on a fruit stall, in a plastic packet, stewed in a saucepan. Other imagery systems in the brain allow us to imagine what an apple would taste like, how it would smell, what it would feel like if touched, what it would sound like if bitten into, and so on. This type of memory for things in the world around us is known as "semantic memory" or "concept memory".

In addition to semantic memory of, for example, an apple, we each have stored in the brain personal memories connected with personal events to do with an apple. For example, I may be able to summon up an image in my head of myself eating an apple for lunch yesterday. This type of personal memory is known as episodic memory. Episodic memory then is memory for episodes that have occurred in an individual's life. Each person's episodic memory store is unique.

Figure 1 on the next page shows how the idea of an apple might be stored in the brain across many different imagery systems.

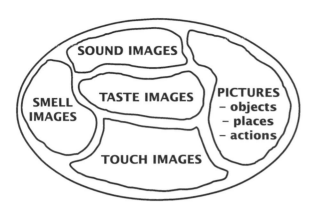

Figure 1: some of the imagery systems that the brain might use in order to store information about things in the world around us and about events that happen to us

To summarise, an idea can be thought of as a collection of non-verbal images in the mind. How then are ideas communicated from one person to another?

COMMUNICATING IDEAS WITH WORDS

One of the most sophisticated ways of communicating ideas is to translate them into words. The following example shows how an idea is communicated from one person to another with words.

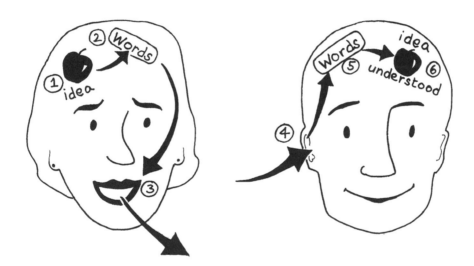

Figure 2: Communicating the idea "I would like an apple"

Stage 1 Non-verbal images form in the mind. The person imagines what an apple tastes like, looks like, feels like, etc. Thinking about the images makes the person decide he wants an apple.

Stage 2 Once the idea has formed, words must be chosen to match that idea. Words are taken from the language area of the brain. This is a kind of mental dictionary where words are attached to non-verbal images.

Stage 3 Once the words which match the person's idea have been chosen in the mind, the brain instructs the muscles of the mouth, throat and chest how to move in order to produce the words ("I would like an apple").

Stage 4 To understand an idea spoken by someone else, the listener must first be able to hear the words.

Stage 5 The words heard are sent to the language area of the brain where they are matched against memories of words.

Stage 6 The words received in the language area are translated into non-verbal images in the listener's mind. Now the listener understands the other person's idea.

COMMUNICATING IDEAS NON-VERBALLY
Although words can convey very complex ideas, non-verbal communication also is important. Non-verbal communication is used at the same time as words to add extra meaning, but it also can be used to convey ideas without words.

Facial Expression
Facial expression is an important non-verbal way of communicating ideas. Sometimes we deliberately alter our facial expressions to communicate a particular message. For example, shop assistants may be taught to smile so as to make customers feel welcome. Sometimes people may be unaware of the effect their facial expressions are having on others. We may avoid a shop where an assistant is unpleasant. He may have said nothing but his facial expressions make us feel we are a nuisance. Our facial expressions communicate feelings such as anger, boredom, pleasure, happiness or sadness. Similarly other people's facial expressions communicate their feelings to us.

"I don't think she likes me."

Eye Contact
Expressions such as *"I could see the anger in his eyes"* or *"She couldn't even look at me"* suggest the importance of eye contact in communicating what people are thinking. We may though be unaware that other people can "read" what we are thinking by observing our eye contact, in just the same way as we read what they are thinking.

Body Language, Gesture and Touch

Sometimes we use body language and gesture to convey a very specific message, for example, nodding or shaking the head for *"yes"* or *"no"*, or shrugging the shoulders for *"I don't know"*. Body language also conveys emotions such as anger or frustration. These may be expressed by waving the fist, physically pushing someone away, or by standing or sitting in a certain position. Emotions such as love and affection may be conveyed with a hug, a kiss, an arm around the shoulder or holding hands.

Emotional Tone of Voice

We learn very early in life to recognise the meaning behind people's emotional tone of voice. Parents may use a gentle, quiet, "sing-song" voice to calm and soothe a baby. A loud, high pitched voice may warn someone of danger. Our tone of voice communicates emotions such as joy, pleasure, happiness, relaxation, fear, anxiety, anger and frustration. We also learn to recognise these emotions in other people's voices.

There are many conditions that could give rise to a breakdown of communication in older people. Different conditions affect different stages of the communication process. These are discussed in the next chapter.

2 Breakdown of communication in older people

• Problems with ideas • Problems with words • Difficulty with moving muscles for speech • Problems with hearing

PROBLEMS WITH IDEAS (see Stages 1 and 6 on page 6)

Problems forming ideas and appreciating the ideas of others occurs in dementing illnesses such as Alzheimer's disease or vascular dementias. Some patients with conditions like stroke, head injury, brain tumour or Parkinson's disease also experience difficulty here. Temporary, sudden confusion (delirium), due for example to a chest infection or urinary tract infection, also can cause problems with ideas, as can depression, isolation or institutionalisation.

Problems with ideas

PROBLEMS WITH WORDS (see Stages 2 and 5 on page 6)
Difficulty thinking of words to match ideas and difficulty understanding the words of others is known as dysphasia or aphasia. It is caused by specific damage to language areas of the brain and may occur in conditions such as stroke, head injury, or brain tumour. People with dementia may have specific problems with words in addition to problems with ideas (page 6, stages 1 and 6). However, for most people with dementia, problems with words usually are much less of an issue than the underlying problem with ideas.

Problems with words

PROBLEMS WITH MOVING MUSCLES FOR SPEECH (see Stage 3 on page 6)
Difficulty with speech because of problems moving the muscles of the mouth to produce words is known as dysarthria. In mild dysarthria, speech might sound slightly slurred. In severe dysarthria the person may be totally unable to move the muscles to produce words. If control of the muscles of the vocal cords is affected, this is known as dyphonia. Dysarthria and dysphonia may occur in conditions such as stroke, head injury or brain tumour, Parkinson's Disease or motor neurone disease. Some patients with dementing illnesses also may have problems here, especially people with a vascular dementia such as multi-infarct dementia.

PROBLEMS WITH HEARING (See Stage 4 on page 6)
Breakdown of communication occurs because the listener cannot hear the speaker's words and therefore does not get the message or mishears and gets the wrong message.

Problems with hearing

3 How does dementia affect verbal communication?

• Problems with ideas • Old memories and new memories • What happens to old memories in dementia? • What happens to new memories in dementia? • Common verbal communication problems in dementia

PROBLEMS WITH IDEAS

The biggest problem for the person with dementia is difficulty forming ideas and appreciating the ideas of others (chapter 2). The mind images that help create an idea in the head do not form easily. The images which do form may be confusing and difficult for the person to make sense of and hold on to. For the person with dementia, trying to hold on to images in the head can be a bit like trying to hold on to a fistful of sand – the images slip out of the mind just as sand slips through the fingers.

The problems with mind images in dementia lead to problems with ideas – that is with thinking, reasoning and making decisions. Most of the communication problems experienced by people with dementia are due to problems with ideas.

For the person with dementia, images which form in the mind can be confusing and hard to make sense of

OLD MEMORIES AND NEW MEMORIES

Chapter 1 showed how an idea in the mind is made up of images created out of old memories of things we have experienced in the past. As we go through each day, we add to the brain's memory store new memories of things we experience. These new memories then become old memories.

What happens to old memories in dementia?

In mild dementia, the person may have little difficulty with old memories from before the onset of dementia. For example, he may have no difficulty remembering what he had for breakfast on the beach in Tenerife twenty years ago. This happens because memories for things that happened before the person developed dementia are already filed away in the brain. They were carefully stored away while the brain was working efficiently (see Figure 1, page 14). (Old memories do however tend to become more affected in more severe dementia.)

What happens to new memories in dementia?

Even in mild dementia, the person may have great difficulty with remembering new experiences. For example, he may be unable to say what he had for breakfast this morning. This happens because there is particular difficulty adding new memories to the memory store. The damaged brain has difficulty holding on to new memories and filing them away for future reference (see Figure 2, page 15). Often the person with dementia has not really "forgotten" what has happened. Instead he did not accurately record the new experience in first place, or did not record it at all.

Which sort of new memories might be easier for the person with dementia?

New experiences that are most likely to be remembered by the person with dementia are those associated with strong emotions, for example, the sad loss of a relative or friend. The emotions help the person to record the event as it happens and to transfer it to the "old memories store".

THE BRAIN WORKING NORMALLY

Figure 1: *The brain working normally*
New memories are sorted out by the brain and put into the old memories "filing cabinet". Old memories can be taken out of the brain's filing cabinet and made into "mind images" when they are needed.

THE PERSON WITH DEMENTIA

Figure 2: *The person with dementia*
The brain finds it difficult to hold on to new experiences and memories. Often they are "dropped" (forgotten) before they can be put into the filing cabinet. Some new memories do make it into the filing cabinet where they become old memories. The person with mild dementia usually has little trouble taking out very old memories from the filing cabinet. As dementia progresses, it becomes harder for the person to find the correct old memories. Also, as dementia worsens, old memories or parts of old memories drop out of the filing cabinet and are lost.

COMMON VERBAL COMMUNICATION PROBLEMS IN DEMENTIA
In a study on communication*, carers of people with dementia were asked about communication difficulties. Commonly reported communication problems were:

- *Asking the same question a number of times*

- *Telling the same story or giving the same piece of information a number of times*

- *Difficulty starting up a conversation and keeping a conversation going*

- *Trouble following a conversation, especially when a group of people are talking.*

- *Drifting from the point during conversation*

- *Difficulty thinking of the names of people, places or objects*

- *Trouble following television programmes*

- *Changing the subject inappropriately*

- *Talking about the past all the time*

- *Starting to say something and then forgetting what he was talking about*

- *Saying he can see things that aren't really there*

- *Saying things that are not true*

Chapter 4 will consider ways of helping people who have these sorts of communication problems.

*Powell JA, Hale MA, Bayer AJ. Symptoms of communication breakdown in dementia: carers' perceptions. *European Journal of Disorders of Communication* 1995; 30: 65-75.

4 Responding to common verbal communication problems in dementia

• A problem solving approach to communication problems • Think: why is this problem happening? • Think: **A** *– Avoid confrontation;* **B** *– Be practical;* **C** *– Clarify the feelings and comfort (if anxious or upset)*

What is the best way of responding to communication problems such as those described in Chapter 3?

There is great variation in the way in which carers respond to individual communication problems. As an example, carers were asked what they do when the person keeps asking the same question a number of times. Below are examples of the range of responses given:

"I keep answering."
"I ignore it."
"I tell her she's already said that."
"For the first five times I answer."
"I tend to walk away.".
"I will get a piece of paper and write it down."
     "I say that I'm not sure."

There is no one right or wrong way of managing communication problems in dementia. However, with trial and error it usually is possible to learn which approach tends to work best for an individual in a particular situation. The following "problem solving" approach to communication problems may help with this.

There is no one right or wrong way of helping – with trial and error it is usually possible to learn which approach works best for an individual in a particular situation

PROBLEM SOLVING APPROACH TO COMMUNICATION PROBLEMS

Think "WHY is this problem happening?"

Understanding WHY something is happening will help the caregiver reason out how it may be best to respond. Most problems can be explained in terms of the difficulty the person has with mind images and memories. Comments or behaviours that seem irrational usually are the person's attempt to make sense of muddled mind images (ideas) that form in the head or to function without the necessary mind images or memories (see Chapters 1, 2 and 3).

It is helpful to keep in mind that, because of their problems with ideas, many people with dementia are unaware that there is anything wrong with them. Try to imagine if someone suddenly started telling you what to do and how to do it or where to go and when. You think you're fine but everyone else keeps interfering. Most of us would be angry, upset and distressed.

Think ABC

The challenge for the caregiver is to offer gentle guidance and almost hidden support so that the person does not feel that their independence is being challenged. The following ABC guidelines should help carers work out how it might be best to respond to problems that arise.

Avoid confrontation

Confronting the person with their mistakes is unlikely to help. It creates a negative atmosphere for no benefit.

Many caregivers describe using a non-committal approach to help keep the peace. This involves giving a non-committal response to mistakes, for example *"Oh really"* or *"I don't know"* rather than using lengthy arguments, discussion or correction. It is, however, important when responding in this way not actively to mislead the person by giving wrong information.

Be practical

It sometimes is possible to anticipate situations that cause problems and to avoid those situations.

When a problem does arise, there may be something practical you can do to ease the situation.

Clarify the feelings and comfort (if anxious or upset)

If the person is anxious or upset, telling him how you think he is feeling may help. You are attempting to clarify his feelings for him. This can help the person feel more at ease (but see page 29 before using this approach).

Examples follow of how the "THINK WHY, THINK ABC" problem-solving approach may be used with specific communication problems.

Problem...

"He asks the same question over and over"

THINK WHY

- The same idea (mind image) keeps forming in the head and he makes it into a question.
- He forgets the answer he has been given.
- He forgets that he has already asked the question.

THINK Ⓐ Ⓑ Ⓒ

Ⓐvoid confrontation

- Don't say: *"You've just asked me that."*
- If practical suggestions such as those below are not working, try a non-committal reply, for example: *"I'm not sure."*

Ⓑe practical

- Try a short simple answer.
- Try writing the answer down for the person to refer to.
- Try avoiding situations that cause repetition; for example, don't mention appointments until the last minute.
- Try distraction – for example, guide towards an activity such as sorting a cutlery drawer or making a cup of tea.

Ⓒlarify the feelings and comfort (if anxious or upset)

- For example: *"You seem worried that you can't remember the date."* (It may be that the fear of not remembering the date is the real issue rather than the date itself.)
- *"I can never remember the date either."*

Problem...

"He says things that are not true"

THINK WHY

- Ideas (mind images) have become mixed up and "fuzzy". Often the mixed-up ideas are to do with time – the past seems like the present.

THINK A B C

Avoid confrontation

- Don't say bluntly *"You don't go to work any more"* if this leads to upset or argument.

Be practical

- Try saying something that incorporates the truth but does not criticise what the person has just said. For example: *"It must be nice being retired. You don't have to get up so early now."* or *"Your job must have been very interesting."*
- Gently and sensitively try changing the subject.
- Try distraction – for example, guide towards an activity: *"Let's make a cup of coffee"* or perhaps *"Let's water the plants".*

Clarify the feelings and comfort (if anxious or upset)

- For example: *"You seem to miss your job. You must have really enjoyed it."*

Problem...

"He has trouble starting up a conversation and keeping a conversation going"

THINK WHY

- Ideas (mind images) are not coming easily into the head.

THINK **A** **B** **C**

Avoid confrontation

- Don't say *"You never talk to me"* or *"Can't you think of something to say?"*

Be practical

- Be prepared to take the lead and start up conversations yourself.
- Try using old memories and universal experiences to stimulate conversation (see Chapter 7)
- Try using a memory album (see Chapter 5)

Clarify the feelings and comfort (if anxious or upset)

- For example, *"It's sometimes hard to think of things to say."*

Problem...

"He has trouble making even simple decisions. Sometimes he can't even decide what we should cook for dinner"

THINK WHY

- Ideas (mind images) of possible meals do not come into the head.
- He has difficulty forming mind images of what's in the fridge or the sequence for preparing and cooking those ingredients.

THINK ABC

Avoid confrontation

- Don't say *"Come on think, what shall we cook?"*

Be practical

- Try making suggestions: *"Shall we cook fish for dinner today? I really fancy some."*

Clarify the feelings and comfort (if anxious or upset)

- For example: *"It's sometimes hard to think of what to cook."*

"He can't stop talking about the past"

THINK WHY

- He has trouble with new memories (see Chapter 3) – without new memories, the mind has only old memories to work with
- He feels safer and more secure when talking about something he remembers well.

THINK A B C

Avoid confrontation

- Don't say *"Not the past again"* or *"We've heard all that before."*
- Try a non-committal response, for example, *"Oh yes"* if you really can't face hearing the story again.

Be practical

- Try to be positive if the person obviously is enjoying talking about the past. If he is muddling past with present, gently try to put what he says into context. For example, *"Yes, that was a long time ago. You were living in Newport then."*
- A memory album or diary can be a useful focus for conversation about the past (see Chapter 5).

Clarify the feelings and comfort (if anxious or upset)

- For example, *"That seems to make you feel sad."*

Problem...

"He starts to say something and then forgets what he was talking about"

THINK WHY

- He has trouble holding on to mind images that form in the head.

THINK

Avoid confrontation

- Don't say: *"You've forgotten again, think."*

Be practical

- Try reminding the person of what he has just said: *"You were telling me about your holiday in Cornwall."*

Clarify the feelings and comfort (if anxious or upset)

- For example: *"It's annoying when that happens isn't it."*

Problem...

"He shouts at me and gets angry with me"

THINK WHY

- Because of difficulty with mind images, reasoning and judgement, he is likely to have trouble seeing things from someone else's point of view. This can lead to misunderstandings.
- This problem often arises where the caregiver has found it difficult to avoid confrontation when dealing with another problem.

THINK A B C

Avoid confrontation

- Try not to take it too personally.
- Try not to think about whose "fault" it is.
- Try to stay calm and let the situation pass – the person himself often quickly forgets the episode.

Be practical

- Anticipate situations that may cause problems. Then try to avoid those situations or find a way around them. For example, if the person keeps wearing a dirty shirt and is upset when you mention it, discreetly replace it with a clean one before he dresses and say nothing.

Clarify the feelings and comfort (if anxious or upset)

- For example: *"I'm sorry you're so angry."*

Problem...

"He calls things by the wrong name"

THINK WHY

- There may be a "short-circuit" in selecting a word to match an idea that forms in the head.
- The idea (mind image) itself may be unclear.

THINK A B C

Avoid confrontation

- Don't draw attention to mistakes – just let them pass.

Be practical

- If the person knows he has used the wrong word, try suggesting the right word.

Clarify the feelings and comfort (if anxious or upset)

- For example: *"Isn't it frustrating when that happens?"*

Problem...

"He struggles to think of the names of things"

THINK WHY

- The person cannot find the correct words to express his idea.

THINK

Avoid confrontation

- Don't say: *"You know the word"* or *"Think harder".*

Be practical

- If you know the word he is struggling to think of, usually it reduces stress if you tell him the word.
- If you don't know what the word is, try "narrowing it down" if this helps and if it reduces frustration. For example, ask, *"Is it something to do with supper?"* or *"Is it something to do with our holiday?"*

Clarify the feelings and comfort (if anxious or upset)

- For example: *"Isn't it frustrating when you can't think of a word?"*

Clarifying the feelings when the person is distressed, anxious or upset (as in the examples just given) involves working out how the person might be feeling in a particular situation and telling him how you think he feels. This can help the person to understand himself which is reassuring. It also can help him feel more at ease because he feels understood.

This approach should, however, be used sensitively. Clarifying a person's feelings sometimes can be unhelpful or inappropriate. If the person seems more at ease when you have suggested how they might be feeling, the approach probably has been appropriate.

It can be a rewarding approach for carers when it is clear that the person has been helped through a difficult situation.

The same clarifying response can be used many times if it helps the person at that moment in time. It can be very repetitive for carers to do this, but it may be the best alternative in terms of quality of life both for the person with dementia and for the carer.

Further examples follow of how the concept of clarifying the feelings could be used in a variety of situations. Of course you also would want to use

A – **Avoid confrontation**

and

B – **Be practical**

in each of these situations too.

Scenario:
A lady is sitting at the breakfast table in a nursing home. Every few minutes she lifts her head and shouts out *"Gran"*, *"Mum"*.

THINK WHY

- Old memories and the concept of time are muddled – the past seems like the present.
- Problems with new memories and ideas mean that she may not know where she is and why she is there.
- She feels lost, disoriented, alone, frightened and confused by a strange environment.

Unhelpful response

Clarify the feelings and comfort

Scenario:
A patient on a hospital ward asks repeatedly *"I want to see the doctor."*

THINK WHY

- Problems with new memories and ideas mean that he may not know where he is or why he is there.
- Problems with new memories mean that he may be forgetting that he is asking the same question repeatedly.
- He may be sensing that all is not well.
- He may think a doctor will allow him to go home.

Unhelpful response

Clarify the feelings and comfort

Scenario:

Two nurses on a hospital ward are sitting in the office discussing the duty roster. A patient repeatedly tries to interrupt and is ignored by staff. Eventually he shouts: *"Why are you ignoring me?"*

THINK WHY

- Problems with mind images, reasoning and thinking things through, make it hard for the person to interpret situations and see things from another point of view. This can make the person with dementia seem self-centred.

Unhelpful response

Clarify the feelings and comfort

The staff are task-oriented and do not make allowances for the illness. The situation could have been avoided if the staff had responded sooner.

Scenario:

A patient on a long-stay hospital ward goes into the office, picks up the waste bin, moves it to another part of the room and empties the contents on the floor.

THINK WHY

- He senses that he should be doing something, but appropriate images of things he could be doing do not form in his head or he does not recognise which of the images that do form are appropriate.
- Images that do form in his head are strong old memories from the past – he used to work as a refuse collector.
- Because of problems with reasoning and thinking things through, he does not realise that the mind images he is acting upon are inappropriate.

Unhelpful response   **C**larify the feelings and comfort

(The patient can gently be guided to another location or activity. Perhaps, he could be guided to help empty all the bins every day at the appropriate time if he enjoys this – but not if it just makes the problem worse and causes repetitive, inappropriate bin emptying).

The above example is interesting. It can be seen that, apart from more obvious reasons for certain behaviour, like restlessness and being unable to think things through, there sometimes is an even more simple explanation behind seemingly meaningless activities. So often the obvious reasons are missed.

5 "Who am I and where have I come from?" Helping communication with memory albums

• What is a memory album? • Encouraging the person with dementia and their family to make a memory album • How to put it together

Each of us holds within our memory a series of key facts about the important people, places and events in our lives. These key facts are "collected" in the mind over the years to form an internal "This is your life" story. This story gives us our "identity". It tells us who we are and allows us to relate to our environment appropriately.

People with dementia may have trouble bringing back information from their life story. Adding new memories and ideas to the story, such as names of new grandchildren, can be particularly difficult. Loss of the ability to remember key facts about ourselves can be disorientating and upsetting. It can seriously affect conversation and communication.

Browsing regularly through a memory album can keep fresh the key facts of the person's life story. This is a boost to their confidence, and can help people feel more relaxed about themselves and their memory

WHAT IS A MEMORY ALBUM?

Just as a walking stick is an aid to walking, a memory album is an aid to memory. It is a record in words and pictures, of the important parts of a person's life, from the beginning right through to the present day. As new life events occur, they can be added to the album.

Browsing regularly through the album can help keep fresh the key facts of the person's life story. This is a boost to the confidence and can help people feel more relaxed about themselves and their memory.

Encouraging the person with dementia and the family to make a memory album

Family members may have difficulty understanding what is happening to their relative and may not see the purpose of a memory album. It is important to have their help and so it is worth taking the time to explain carefully what a memory album is and how it can be useful. It is, of course, also important to "sell" the idea to the person with dementia, especially if he is only mildly impaired.

It is helpful to explain that when people have trouble with their memory, they sometimes have difficulty remembering names, places, dates and so on. Mention how frustrating this can be. Explain that there is something that can be done to help with this. When someone has problems with their sight they use a visual aid, for example, glasses. If they have trouble walking they may use a walking aid, for example a walking stick. If they have trouble with their memory they could use a memory aid. One type of memory aid is a memory album.

A visual demonstration is important for conveying the concept of a memory album. If possible, show an example of a memory album – you can make a demonstration album yourself using photographs or pictures from magazines. Seeing someone's life history presented in this way seems to encourage families to have a go at putting together an album for their relative.

How could a memory album be put together?

A 6" by 4" photo album with plastic pockets for about 36 pictures makes and ideal memory album. This is easy to carry around and is generally acceptable as it resembles more traditional memory aids such as diaries and notebooks.

For people with more severe dementia, a larger album allows the use of larger photographs and captions which may be recognised more easily. Remember though that some people with dementia are no longer able to recognise pictures or understand what they mean. It is, however, still worth making an album for that person – the album will help those involved in the person's care to see him as an individual.

If you are using a six by four inch photo album, first slip a piece of paper six inches by four inches inside each pocket of the album. On some pages write about the person's life. On other pages, use the piece of paper as a backing for photographs leaving room to write captions describing the photo. Write with clear lettering, avoiding capitals (as in the examples that follow). Newspaper cuttings of relevant places or events in the person's life could also be included in the album.

Try to start at the beginning of the person's life with facts about where the person was born and when. Continue right through to the present day. Sample pages for a memory album follow, to give an idea of the sort of things that could be included.

George Evans.
I was born on 25th
July 1932 in
Fairland
Cardiff.

This was me aged about 2 years

My parents were Jack and
Charlotte Evans.

My father owned a
gentleman's outfitters
in Cardiff.

My parents Charlotte and Jack
Evans in the 1940's

I was one of 4 children.
My brother Ernie is 2 years
older.
My sister Mary is 3 years
older.
Sadly my younger sister
June died a long time ago
when she was 22.

Mary, June, me and Ernie
at Barry Island in the 1940's

During my childhood I lived in Wake Avenue, Fairland, Cardiff.

Later we moved to Burlock. 88 Hillside Road.

our old childhood home in Burlock

I left school when I was 14 years old.

when I first left school I worked in a local baker's shop.

When I was 16, I started work as an apprentice to a plumber.

Me, in about 1948 soon after starting work as a plumber.

My wife's name is Mavis.

We met at a dance in the old Ballroom in Queen Street, Cardiff.

Mavis and Me in 1955

We had just got engaged.

We were married on
15th June, 1957
at St. Catherine's Church
in Penlark, Cardiff.

My brother Ernie was my
best man.
Mavis' sister Enid was her
bridesmaid.

our Wedding in 1957.

When we were first married we
lived in Riseland Road, Cardiff.

We have also lived in Windor
Place, Salway Cardiff.

Our address is now
10 Oaklane Close,
Meadowvale,
Cardiff.

Mavis and me outside our
bungalow in Oaklane Close.
We moved here when I retired
in 1997.

I had one child, Carol
who was born on
18th May 1961.
This is her when
she was 2 years old
on holiday in Tenby.

My daughter Carol on the beach
in Tenby ~ aged 2 years.

My daughter Carol is now married to Mark.
They live in Reading.
They have 3 children.
Alice was born in 1985.
Hugh was born in 1987.
Lucy was born in 1995.

Dad, Mum, Lucy, Alice and Hugh, Reading 1995.

I worked until I was 65.
Most of my working life I worked as an engineer. The last job I had before retiring was with Jones Engineering in the docks.

Me at my retirement party in 1997. It was held at the Parkland Hotel.

My brother Ernie now lives in Gloucester with his wife Freda.

Freda and Ernie outside their home in Gloucester. Summer 1997.

My sister Mary now lives in Bristol.

Her husband, Eric, died a few years ago.

A recent photo of Mary with me. We were on holiday in Tenerife.

I go bowling every Friday at the club in Harbourend Road, Penark.

Mavis makes the tea!

My wife Mavis.

Me, bowling with my friends at the club.

Peter   Dorothy

Our good friends from Oaklane Close Sully. Photo taken a few years ago.

Our best friend, Apricot our alsation! he's now about 7 years old.

As shown above, each photograph should be described with enough information to allow someone who has never seen the photograph to know who is in it, where it was taken and when. For example, the caption "Carol" would be too limited, whereas the caption "My daughter Carol on the beach in Tenby aged 2 years" would be about right. It reminds the person with memory problems that he has a daughter who is called Carol and that when Carol was very small the family went on holiday to Tenby. An added benefit of writing such detailed information is that it avoids embarrassment and frustration when someone looking through the album asks who Carol is or where the photo was taken and the person with memory problems has forgotten.

The captions describing the photos should use adult language. A useful guideline is to ask yourself if it would be acceptable to you.

Making a memory album can be an enjoyable hobby. It can be created a little bit at a time. Once you have built up the main part of the album, remember to add new events that happen. For people who move to residential care, it could be useful to include photographs (with appropriate captions) of the outside and inside of the building, along with photographs of staff and significant fellow residents, for example roommates.

Getting started on a memory album

At the end of this book (p.92 onwards) is a set of pre-printed pages that can be photocopied and cut up for use in a 6" by 4" photo album. These could be a useful starting point for an album. Space is left on each page for filling in relevant information before inserting into the album with appropriate photographs.

Using a memory album for specific problems

–	If someone has difficulty recognising a family member, a set of photographs of that person at different ages could be included in the album. For example the following captions could accompany appropriate photographs, as in the examples overleaf:

My husband Jack on our wedding day in 1960.

This was taken a long time ago when Jack was a young man of 28.

My husband Jack on his 40th birthday in 1972.

Jack and me at our Silver Wedding in 1985. Jack was then 53 years old.

My husband Jack and Me on holiday in Tenby last year.

Similarly, if someone continually says that his home is not really where he lives, the following series could be included in the album:

Our old home in Swansea.

We lived here for 32 years.

28 Rockland Road, Cardiff. This is where we live now. We moved here 5 years ago in 1992.

Using a memory album

• The person with dementia may forget to look at the album regularly. Try to encourage him to do so in order to keep the memories fresh.

• Leave the album out for example in the living room so it is always on hand.

• The album can be a good focus for conversation for visitors and especially for grandchildren.

• Remember to add new events to the album as they happen.

Potential benefits of using a memory album

• Keeps "key facts" fresh – helping to preserve them in memory for as long as possible.

• Helps maintain a sense of identity – offers a sense of security of knowing oneself.

• Builds self-esteem and confidence.

• Makes the person feel his life is of value.

• Provides a focus for conversation.

• Allows the person to take the lead in conversation.

• Can offer people with mild dementia a method of self-prompting during conversation.

• Provides opportunity for life review.

• Allows people to focus on the good times.

• Offers a sense of security when the person moves on to day care or permanent care.

• Helps staff to see the person as an individual.

• Provides staff with ideas for stimulating conversation.

• Encourages personalised care in long stay institutions.

OTHER IDEAS TO HELP KEEP PEOPLE'S NAMES, FACES AND PLACES "FRESH" IN THE MEMORY:

• Make an "Important People" picture, put it in a clip-frame and hang it on the wall.

• Make a "family tree" for each branch of the family and put each one in a separate clip frame. For example, one clip frame with the person's son and his family, another with the person's daughter and her family. Ask family members to help.

• Make an "Important Places" picture, put it in a clip-frame and hang it on the wall. This could show clearly labelled photographs of the person's home, social club, daughter's home, etc.

6 "What should I do and how do I do it?" A structured and guided day

• Helping the person with dementia to plan and organise their day – deciding "What should I do?" and "How do I do it?" • Structuring the day with lists and timetables • Guiding the person through a task

Memory albums (Chapter 5) help keep memories of important people, places and events fresh. These memories allow us to know "who am I and where have I come from?".

To feel secure and confident we also need to be able to decide "What should I do?" and "How do I do it?". This means organising ourself from day-to-day, remembering what to do next and planning how to do it.

The person with dementia may have trouble planning his day. This is because of problems with forming ideas, reasoning and thinking things through. He may be aware that he should be doing something but does not know what. Ideas (mind images) of possible things he could be doing just do not come into his head. If an idea does come, he may have trouble thinking how to put the idea into action. Even ideas that seem simple can be difficult. For example, planning how to go about vacuuming a room can be a major problem for the person with dementia.

Problems with knowing what to do and how to do it can lead to restlessness and to feelings of uselessness and despair. Alternatively the person may sit and do nothing. This can give the appearance of withdrawal or depression. Remember too that it is important for all us to feel useful. (But also remember that there are times when we *need* to sit and do nothing in order to relax.)

Problems with knowing what to do and how to do it can lead to restlessness and despair – remember that it is important for all of us to feel useful

Usually the person himself is unable to describe what it feels like when he does not know what he should be doing. The following quote from someone with dementia gives a rare insight into what may be happening.

"I woke up and got myself in a state. I couldn't remember who or what I was. I remembered my name but couldn't think what I was doing there."

"At home I'm not doing as much as I'd like to. There's work I should be doing but I can't seem to get myself motivated to do the things I'd like to do."

Q: *"What would you like to do?"*

"I haven't given it a thought. I wash the dishes, dry the dishes, clean the windows. Not of my own doing you understand. My wife says, 'You look lost'. She realises I'm in a state. I need to have my hands doing something. It takes the strain off my memory box."

WHAT SHOULD I DO? – STRUCTURING THE DAY WITH LISTS
Some people have found that it helps to structure the day with a "Things to Do Today" list. A carer could sit with the person each morning, or the night before, and between them they could write a list of activities for the day (see below). This helps get around the problem the person has with forming mind images of possible things he could be doing.

The list should be kept in a prominent position, for example, stuck to a door. The person is likely to need reminding to check the list from time to time during the day and especially when he seems to be "at a loss".

Monday things to do ~

- Sweep the back path
- Walk to post office with Enid to get our pensions.
- Practice my golf putting indoors if it rains.
- Clean the downstairs windows inside.
- Watch the snooker.

Suggestions for "Things to Do Today" list

Household jobs
> Sweep the path
> Hang out the washing
> Plant the bulbs
> Clean the shoes
> Polish the silver

Leisure Activities
> Go swimming
> Practice indoor golf putting
> Challenge Enid to Bagatelle
> Feed the ducks
> Watch the ice-skating video

The most successful activities usually are those which put fewer demands on complex thinking and reasoning skills. It is a challenge to find enjoyable activities that make use of simple, well-learned repetitive sequences.

The Dementia Services Development Centre, Stirling University, produces several helpful publications on activities for people with dementia, both in their own home and in a residential or day care environment.*

POTENTIAL BENEFITS OF USING A "THINGS TO DO TODAY LIST"

• Provides a structure to day-to-day life

• Promotes a sense of confidence and security

• Builds feelings of self-worth by giving the person a purpose to each day

• Can help carers to manage restlessness

• Reassures the person that he can relax when all the tasks are checked off

• Helps with orientation by allowing the person to look back and see what has been happening and what is about to happen.

---

* *Activities* by Carole Archibald. Describes how activities can enhance the quality of life of staff and people with dementia. £6.00.
Activities II by Carole Archibald. Focuses on activities for men, for those in the last stages of dementia and as a means of managing difficult behaviour. £8.50.
Activities and people with dementia: Involving family carers by Carole Archibald and Charlie Murphy (editors). £8.50.
All available from Dementia Services Development Centre, University of Stirling, Stirling FK9 4LA. Tel 01786 467740, fax 01786 466846. Special offers (two publications for £12, all three for £18) may apply.

HOW DO I DO IT? – GUIDING THE PERSON THROUGH A TASK

Sometimes, just reminding the person to check the list will be enough to start him off on an appropriate task. Others will need a little more prompting to get them going on a task. For example, if the list says "Do the vacuuming" you may need to prompt: *"We need to take the vacuum out of the cupboard under the stairs."* The person may then be able to carry out the task with no further guidance.

Some people, however, will need a lot of guidance throughout a task. This is because tasks that seem simple can, in fact, require a great deal of mind imagery, thinking and planning. For example, to carry out a task like vacuuming, the person would need to be able to form in his head a series of mind images of how this task should be done. He would need to imagine in his head what the vacuum cleaner looks like and where it is kept. He would need to imagine himself unravelling the cable, plugging the plug in the electric socket, switching the vacuum on and moving the vacuum through the house.

The carer may need to guide the person through every step of a task. For example:

"Let's do the vacuuming"

> *"We need to take the vacuum cleaner out from under the stairs."*

When this is done, continue:

> *"We need to unwind the cable."*

When this is done, continue:

> *"It plugs in over here."*

When this is done, continue:

> *"Let's vacuum the living room."*   etc...

Use phrases like:	*Avoid phrases like:*
Let's do the vacuuming	*Why don't you* do the vacuuming
We need to do the vacuuming	*Go and do* the vacuuming
Would you help me with vacuuming	

None of us likes being told what to do!

This method of providing step-by-step guidance can be used with any task – washing the dishes, dressing, washing, etc. The step-by-step approach can, of course, be used even if you decide not to use a "Things to do Today" list.

Guiding the person in this way can be time-consuming and requires patience. For this reason, it is not always practical to involve the person with dementia in some tasks. However, wherever possible, the person should be encouraged to become involved with any tasks he enjoys.

WHAT SHOULD I DO? – STRUCTURING THE DAY WITH TIMETABLES
Some people, especially those with mild dementia, find it helpful to use a weekly planner/timetable. There is a blank copy of a weekly planner/timetable, which can be photocopied, on p91. Alternatively you could use a wipe-clean board.

The month and date should be written below each day, and the year can be entered at the top of the sheet. The sort of things to include on the timetable and the amount of detail would vary from one person to another.

Suggestions for timetables

Appointments
> 11 o'clock hairdresser
> 3.30 meet John at the club
> 7.30 Hilary coming for coffee

Day-to-day affairs
> Phone optician to make appointment
> Buy toothpaste
> Post Peter's birthday card
> Collect prescription from the doctor's surgery

The timetable should be pinned in a prominent position, for example to the kitchen or living room wall, so that it can checked whenever necessary.

People differ in their ability to use timetables. Some people regard their timetables as "mission control". Others do not take to them at all. Those who do find them helpful are likely to need a lot of help with updating. Also they will need to be reminded to use them.

Timetables can help people feel more in control of their life and help maintain confidence and a sense of purpose. They can help those living alone to cope in their own home, especially if introduced early in the illness.

WHAT SHOULD I DO? USING A DESK DIARY
Some people like to use a desk diary. As with timetables, a diary can be particularly helpful for those with mild problems.

The person may benefit from writing in their diary things that have happened, as well as things that are going to happen. For example, a diary entry may record that the person is due to attend a hospital appointment On returning from the appointment, the person could be encouraged to write down what happened at the appointment, what the doctor's name was and so on. Writing things down can help those with mild dementia remember things they may otherwise forget. Also, the person can look back over the record of events.

The person may need to be prompted to write in the diary regularly. He also may need to be encouraged to check the diary during the day and perhaps especially first thing in the morning, maybe before or during breakfast. He also should be encouraged to keep the diary in one place, for example by the phone. It may be best to keep it open at the right page.

7 Helping communication with old memories and universal experiences

• General guidelines to encourage conversation • Using old memories and universal experiences

Conversation with a person with dementia can be easier if topics are introduced that draw on the person's strengths and avoid their weaknesses.

GENERAL GUIDELINES TO ENHANCE CONVERSATION

In Chapter 3 we looked at the difference between new memories and old memories. The person with dementia has problems getting new experiences that happen into the old memories "filing cabinet". Memories put into the filing cabinet before the person developed dementia are more likely to be retained. Often, though, the person may need prompting to take old memory files out of the filing cabinet. Keeping in mind the type of memories that are hardest and easiest for the person with dementia, try the following:

It helps to draw on the person's strengths and avoid their weaknesses – so tap into old memories, using feelings and situations that we have all experienced and understand (memories of schooldays, play, first job...)

DON'T keep asking the person questions that rely on new memories. For example, *"What did you have for breakfast?"*, *"How old is your grand-daughter now?"*, *"When are you going on holiday?"*. Of course questions like this will crop up automatically in conversation from time to time, but it is good to be aware that these are the sorts of questions that can be conversation stoppers.

DO tap into the person's old memories. However, be careful with this – certain old memories may be unpleasant for some people.

In Chapters 2 and 3, we looked at how problems with ideas leads to problems with thinking things through and reasoning things out. Because of this:

DON'T use topics that are intellectually demanding.

DO tap into feelings and situations that are universal, that is tap into feelings and situations we have all experienced and understand.

To summarise, try to stimulate old memories and use universal feelings and experiences.

USING OLD MEMORIES AND UNIVERSAL EXPERIENCES – IDEAS FOR TOPICS TO STIMULATE CONVERSATION

Below are just a few ideas for topics to help conversation. The range of possible topics is, of course, endless.

Childhood has some of the most powerful memories, especially those connected with school, friends and discipline and with important emotional events.

Childhood – behaviour

- *Were you a bad child or a good child?*

- *What made you behave?*

- *What was the naughtiest thing you ever did?*

- *What sort of punishment did you have?*

- *Did you do anything dangerous that your parents never knew about?*

Childhood – school and friends

- *Did you have a favourite teacher? Why was he/she your favourite?*

- *Was there a teacher you really disliked? Why?*

- *Did you have a best friend?*

- *Do you remember anyone being bullied?*

Childhood – important events

- *Did you ever get lost when you were a child?*

- *Did you ever have to go into hospital?*

- *Can you remember being so excited that you couldn't sleep? When was that?*

- *Do you remember having a special outfit for parties and special occasions?*

Childhood – play

- *What did you wear to go swimming?*

- *What were your favourite games?*

- *Were you allowed to have pets? Which one was most important to you?*

- *Did you ever collect anything when you were a child?*

- *Did you have a favourite toy. Do you remember what happened to it?*

Childhood – fears

- *Were you afraid of the dark when you were a child?*

- *Were you afraid of spiders or snakes? Are you still afraid now?*

- *Did you go to the dentist when you were a child? Were you afraid? Are you still afraid now?*

Young adulthood usually is a time of turning points, decisions and important emotional events.

Young adulthood – work

- *How did you feel about leaving school?*

- *What was your first job?*

- *How much did you earn in your first job? What happened to your first wage packet?*

Young adulthood – social

- *Where did you go for a good night out?*

- *Can you remember your first girlfriend/boyfriend?*

Topics such as these can spark off long discussions. They also work well in a group because they involve emotions with which everyone can identify. In addition, the intellectual and reasoning skills required are relatively simple.

Visitors can be encouraged to start conversation around these sorts of topics. For example, perhaps suggest to grandchildren that they ask grandad about the naughtiest thing he did when he was a child.

One or two postcards, photos or magazine clippings can provide a useful starting point for discussion. For example, pictures of modern bridal wear cut from magazines could lead on to a discussion about the sort of outfits worn years ago.

Materials are available commercially, but usually it is better to gather together your own using local sources. Try also to use photos and other personal mementos of the person with whom you are working.

A Pocket Book of Memories, produced by Hawker Publications, is a useful aid (in filofax format and lively presentation), to stimulating conversation through reminders of personal memories.*

* *A Pocket Book of Memories* by Linda Sheppard and Jenny Rusted. Available price £9.99 from Hawker Publications, tel 020 7720 2108, fax 020 7498 3023.

8 Helping communication with television and video

• Why does the person have trouble watching television? How carers can help • Using videos – "Video therapy"

TV programmes with music, scenery, strong colours, mood and atmosphere may be enjoyed. Wildlife programmes, some comedy programmes, some sports programmes or those with singing or dancing may also be successful.

Watching television is a popular and relaxing pastime. Some people with dementia continue to watch and enjoy television as much as ever, but may quickly forget what they have just watched. Carers sometimes worry about this. They may feel that it is a waste of time the person watching television if they can not remember what they have just watched. This is not true. All of us quickly forget most of what we have watched on the television. The person with dementia simply forgets a little bit sooner. The important thing is that we enjoyed it at the time – it's the present moment that counts. Also, the effects of the enjoyment of the present moment will be absorbed subconsciously. This encourages feelings of well-being.

Some people have trouble sitting and looking at television for any length of time. They may say it is rubbish, they may keep talking or asking questions or they may be restless or fidgety. For the family caregiver, this can be a problem because it makes it difficult to relax at the end of a busy day. Also, the carer may feel that the person is not enjoying life as much as he could if he were able to sit and look at television for longer.

WHY DOES THE PERSON HAVE TROUBLE SITTING AND LOOKING AT TELEVISION? – HOW CAN I HELP?

- Some programmes require a lot of concentration on what is being said. People with dementia often have trouble concentrating.

  You can help by choosing programmes with fewer words or with words spoken slowly and clearly.

- Enjoyment of the programme may rely on the person remembering something that happened earlier.

  You can help by choosing programmes that do not rely heavily on remembering what has just happened.

- Some programmes require a lot of logic and reasoning.

  You can help by choosing programmes that are relatively simple and do not involve a lot of complicated reasoning.

- Enjoyment of the programme may require the person to anticipate what might happen. People with dementia have trouble imagining the future and what might happen.

  You can help by choosing programmes that do not need anticipation of the future. Instead, look for programmes that have "pleasure in the moment".

To help overcome the problems described above, consider trying programmes with music, scenery, strong colours, mood and atmosphere. Wild-life programmes, some comedy programmes, some sports programmes or programmes with singing or dancing may be successful.

Observing the person's response to different kinds of programmes will help you understand what the person can watch and enjoy best.

USING VIDEOS – "VIDEO THERAPY"

If you find that the person likes certain programmes, you can record these onto a video and use them again. Do not assume that because the person has seen a programme once that he will not want to see it again. In fact, it is no different from listening to the same music tape or CD again. If the person enjoys it, use it as a form of therapy.

Pre-recorded videos also may be enjoyed. A few hours spent searching through a good specialist videotape store which has a hobbies/special interest section can turn up excellent material at reasonable cost. For example:

- A video of "100 Best Goals" may be enjoyed by someone who likes football, but cannot concentrate on the less interesting parts of a match.

- A video of clips of "talented pets" can be fun for the animal lover. It is strongly visual, humorous and gives pleasure in each moment.

- A video of stories from the Bible narrated with a backdrop of stained-glass windows may be enjoyed by some. It is visually stimulating, moves slowly and has familiar words which can be comforting.

- A video of countryside scenery with relaxing music may be enjoyed. It can be soothing for people who are restless.

A WORD OF CAUTION...

For some people, television can have a disturbing effect. They may, for example, believe that people on the television are in the room with them. If television is upsetting, it should be avoided. However, you may notice that only certain programmes have this effect. If so, you need only avoid those particular programmes. Also consider trying different programmes. For example, some people who are restless or who can not cope with programmes with people and words may find it relaxing to watch a video of gentle music with countryside scenery. It is worth a try, but be prepared to switch off if it is a problem.

9 Helping with difficulty in understanding

- *Think about hearing* • *Think about vision*
- *Change the environment* • *Change the way you speak*

Don't ask questions while you are running around doing other things or have your head turned away. Do turn off background noises such as radio or TV, and wait until you have eye contact with the person before you speak.

TO HELP UNDERSTANDING – THINK ABOUT HEARING

Problems with hearing inevitably affect the ability to understand. The person with dementia will have particular difficulty compensating for a hearing loss and will need help to do so (see Chapter 10).

TO HELP UNDERSTANDING – THINK ABOUT VISION

A common observation made by people who wear glasses is that they can hear better with their glasses on. Surprisingly, this can be true because we use lip reading and non-verbal communication to help us to understand and "hear" the message.

The person with dementia may need to be reminded to wear his glasses at the appropriate times. Also, he may be unable to work out that his glasses are dirty and may need your guidance with this.

TO HELP UNDERSTANDING – CHANGE THE ENVIRONMENT

DON'T   Ask questions while you are running around doing other things and when you have your head turned away.

DO   Turn off background noises such as the radio or TV. This will make conversations much easier.

DO   Wait until you have eye-contact with the person before you speak. Calling his name and touching him on the arm can help with this.

DO   Sit or stand close to the person, either in front of him or next to him. This allows you to be seen and heard more clearly.

TO HELP UNDERSTANDING – CHANGE THE WAY YOU SPEAK

DO   Use short, simple sentences.

DO   Emphasise important words.

For example:
*"I've made your **favourite cake**."*

DO   Speak clearly.

DO   Give time for each short sentence to get through.

DO   Repeat if it seems the person has not understood.

DON'T Use too many words.

DON'T Speak too quickly.

DO   Point to an object or person when you mention them. For example, show the person the cake.

DO   Try to avoid questions that need the person to think up possible answers by himself. Also try not to give too many choices in one question. Questions requiring a simple *"yes"* or *"no"* answer are often best, for example: *"Would you like coffee?"*

DO   Use concrete words, for example, *"get married"* rather than *"tie the knot"*, *"It's raining hard"* rather than *"It's raining cats and dogs"*. People with dementia can sometimes take things literally!

DO   Tell the person what you are going to be talking about if the idea is quite long or a bit complicated. For example, *"I want to talk to you about your daughter."* This "sets the scene" and helps the person to "tune in".

DO   Use "memory reminders". As you go along, use reminders of who people are and where places are (see example that follows).

Example

"Jim"

- *touch arm*
- *try to get eye contact*
- *repeat if necessary*

"I'm going to tell you about John"

- *pause,*
- *repeat if necessary*
- *could show photograph of John*

"Your nephew, John"

"He's getting married tomorrow"

- *pause*
- *repeat if necessary*

"His wife is Rachel"

- *pause*
- *repeat if necessary*

"They're getting married in St Catherine's Church"

- *pause*
- *repeat if necessary*

"St Catherine's Church is in Kings Road, Fairwater"

- *pause*
- *repeat if necessary*

This example is much better than saying:

"You won't believe it but John and Rachel are getting married in the church round the corner in the morning."

10 Hearing loss and dementia

• *Why compensating for hearing loss and coping with a hearing aid, is much harder for the person with dementia* • *Hints for talking to people who have a hearing loss*

A hearing loss that occurs in many elderly people is known as *presbyacusis.* In this condition, the ability to hear high-frequency sounds like "s", "t" and "k" is most affected. Words sound "muffled" to the person with this sort of hearing loss. They are therefore hard to distinguish.

Other causes of deafness in elderly people include tinnitus (noises in the ear with no external source) and otosclerosis (thickening of the tissues and bones within the ear). Another kind of hearing loss is caused by a build-up of wax in the ears. This is known as a conductive hearing loss and can be treated by syringing of the ears by the family doctor or other specialist.

Anyone who has a hearing loss needs to learn to compensate for the loss. When thinking and memory are normal, it is not too difficult to learn to do this. The person with a normal memory remembers that he has a hearing loss. He usually knows when he has not heard correctly and can think clearly about what to do about this. For example, he may say that he has not heard and ask the speaker to repeat.

The person with dementia who has a hearing loss may forget that he has a hearing problem. He may not realise he has not heard and may therefore not ask you to repeat.

COPING WITH HEARING LOSS IN DEMENTIA

The person with dementia is likely to have some difficulty compensating for hearing loss because of problems with reasoning and thinking things through.

The person with dementia who has a hearing loss...

... may forget that he has a hearing problem

... may not realise that he has not heard and therefore may not compensate by asking you to repeat.

COPING WITH A HEARING AID IN DEMENTIA

The person with dementia who has a hearing aid...

> ... will have particular difficulty learning to use a hearing aid for the first time

> ... will need help to keep his hearing aid clean, free from wax and in good working order

> ... may not realise that his aid is not working or that it is blocked with wax. He may be unaware that it is just sitting in his ear making hearing problems even worse.

> ... may forget how to adjust his hearing aid correctly for different situations (eg. which volume setting he should use for one-to-one conversation and which for walking outside in traffic).

> ... may not be able to let you know that his hearing aid is set too loudly or that it is "squeaking". He may not realise why he feels so uncomfortable. (You will need to be aware of this. It can be distressing to be left with an aid in the ear under these circumstances).

**Remember –
A non-functioning hearing aid, or an aid that is blocked with wax, simply acts as an ear-plug and makes hearing problems much worse!**

If the person does not have a hearing aid or refuses to wear the aid even though it is working, a converser* may make one-to-one conversation easier. A converser consists of a small box with microphone and a lead running to lightweight headphones. It looks a bit like a Walkman! A similar system is available for use with a television set.

One benefit of a converser is that the microphone can be directed towards the person speaking. In contrast, hearing aids will amplify all noises equally (including footsteps, cars, meal trolleys etc). This could be confusing to the person with dementia who may have particular difficulty filtering out irrelevant sounds and concentrating on those that matter.

If you try a converser*, you will need carefully to observe the person's reactions to see if it helps.

*Converser and television aid available from Sarabec Limited, 15 High Force Road, Middlesbrough TS2 1RH, tel 01642 247789, or ask your local audiology department.

HINTS FOR TALKING TO PEOPLE WHO HAVE A HEARING LOSS

DO   Eliminate noisy distractions such as the TV, radio, outside noise.

DO   Sit or stand close to the person, preferably in front of him. This allows you to be seen and heard more clearly.

DO   Sit or stand with the light in your face when you are speaking so that the person can see your mouth and facial expressions.

DO   Make sure that the person is wearing the appropriate glasses and that they are clean.

DO   Get the person's attention before you speak, for example by touching him on the arm.

DO Speak clearly

DO Watch to see if the person has understood and repeat if it seems necessary.

DO Rephrase as needed. For example the person may not understand *"What's your address"* but may be able to understand *"Where do you live"* (or vice versa).

DON'T Speak too quickly.

DON'T Shout. Shouting distorts words and makes them harder to understand.

Raising your voice *a little* may help.

DON'T Exaggerate your mouth movements. This makes it harder to lip read because it changes the way the words "look".

DON'T Hide your mouth while you are talking. For example don't hide behind a newspaper or put your hand over your mouth.

11 Helping communication – the physical environment

- *Ideas for adapting the environment to make it less confusing: remove unnecessary clutter; try labelling; improve lighting...*
- *Try to create an environment that gently stimulates all the senses*

Any changes should be kept to a minimum. However, the environment can carefully be adapted to help the person feel more at ease and provide the right kind of stimulation.

Changes within the physical environment can be confusing for the person with dementia. This is because of the difficulty the person has with learning new information (see chapter 3).

For many carers, this problem of coping with changes to the environment first becomes obvious when on holiday. The person suddenly is in a totally new environment and has no old memories of the place to help him find his way around. The person may therefore have trouble remembering where his hotel room is or may have difficulty finding the toilet in his room.

As dementia progresses, it becomes more important to think about the physical environment. Any changes should be kept to a minimum. The environment can, however, carefully be adapted to help the person feel more at ease and to provide an appropriate degree of stimulation.

IDEAS FOR ADAPTING THE ENVIRONMENT
Below are a few ideas for creating a user-friendly environment. As always you will need to be selective as not all the ideas will be appropriate for everybody. Also, some of the ideas are really more suited to people in a group home or ward rather than in their own home.

- Regularly remove unnecessary clutter so that it is easier for the person to find the things needed to carry out activities of daily life. For example, only keep on the dressing table the items the person needs to use there. Put ornaments on a shelf instead.

- Try labelling the environment, for example with pictures and words on a cupboard door to show what's inside.

- Make sure that lighting is good so that the chances of the person misperceiving things is reduced. At night, shadows in the corner of a poorly lit room may be confusing.

- Try leaving a light on all night if the person tends to become confused or disoriented when getting up to use the toilet.

- Try leaving doors open if the person has trouble finding their way to the correct room.

- Brightly coloured tape on edges of steps can help prevent falls.

• Use bright colours on bathroom and toilet doors. Although new learning is likely to be a problem for the person with dementia, using constant verbal reinforcement sometimes can help the person to learn new things, for example, *"Do you need the bathroom? That's the red door."* It is worth having a go at helping the person to learn important things like this.

• A flowery border strip pasted to the wall can act as a "trail" for the person to follow to find the toilet. Use gentle prompts and reinforcement; for example, *"Follow the flowers".*

• Place a photo and name on the person's bedroom door if they have trouble finding their bedroom. Help them to find their room by guiding them to the door with their photo and name. It is possible they may be able to learn this important task if given gentle encouragement and repetition.

• Use strong, bright colours for furniture and fabrics but avoid patterns. Patterns can be confusing for the person with dementia. For example, they may interpret a pattern on a carpet as little insects crawling around. On the other hand, bright, plain fabrics and surfaces can help some people recognise things more easily.

• Create an environment that gently stimulates all the senses. This sometimes is known as a multi-sensory environment. It should offer opportunities for stimulating hearing, touch, smell and vision (see also Chapter 13).

- Position a chair or dining table near a window where for example a street scene or bird table can be observed as well as the weather and change in the seasons.

- Use seasonal decorations inside to create the mood of the seasons outside.

- Mirrors sometimes cause people distress because they are having trouble recognising themselves. The individual may be upset by being stared at by this "other" person. Cover up or remove mirrors if they are a problem.

- A mirror on the back of a door or disguising doors in some other way (with a heavy curtain, for example) can discourage wandering if the person tends to do this.

- Limit unnecessary noise and clatter. People with dementia can be highly sensitive to sound. Remember that the person may be unable to let you know that the sounds are uncomfortable for him. He may not even know himself why it feels so bad.

- A rummage area full of bits and pieces may help people who are restless.

12 Quality of life in more severe dementia: non-verbal communication

• *Think about what the person with dementia and you are communicating non-verbally to each other*

A common thread running through this book so far has been the importance of using and understanding non-verbal communication. When helping the person with more severe dementia it is vital that the caregiver's non-verbal communication skills are used to the full.

The person with more severe dementia is likely to have problems telling people about even his most basic needs and feelings. He will be relying on caregivers to learn to understand his non-verbal communication in order to help him achieve the best possible quality of life.

THINK ABOUT WHAT THE PERSON IS COMMUNICATING NON-VERBALLY TO YOU

You may know already that the person uses a certain facial expression, emotional tone of voice, body posture, gesture or a certain look in the eye to mean something in particular (see also Chapter 1). Build on this knowledge to try and understand what he is communicating. Learn to recognise what causes reactions such as pleasure, relaxation or annoyance.

THINK ABOUT WHAT YOU ARE COMMUNICATING NON-VERBALLY

The caregiver also will need to learn to be aware of his own non-verbal messages (see Chapter 1). Remember that you can transmit your feelings of annoyance, anger and frustration without even being aware that this is happening.

As you begin to understand your own non-verbal communication, you can start to use it more consciously in a positive way. For example, you can use your facial expressions, eye contact, body language and emotional tone of voice to convey your interest, care and concern or to have a calming effect.

A particularly good time consciously to use your own non-verbal communication skills is when helping the person with daily care activities. So often these activities are carried out in a rushed "let's get it over with" manner. So many opportunities to meet the individual at a one-to-one level are wasted.

You can use your facial expressions, eye contact, body language and emotional tone of voice to convey your interest, care and concern or to have a calming effect. A good time to use these skills is when helping the person with daily care activities.

The rewards of using non-verbal communication both for the person with dementia and the carer can be great. The challenge for the carer is to recognise the opportunities and have a go.

The next chapter will consider how non-verbal communication could be recorded formally in order to help achieve best possible quality of life for an individual.

13 Quality of life in more severe dementia: stimulation and activities

• *Achieving the right level of stimulation and activity is very important: too little can lead to apathy and withdrawal; too much can cause anxiety and panic* • *Incorporating simple levels of stimulation into daily care actvities in a creative way* • *Using the CLIPPER*

The person with dementia cannot help himself to even simple pleasures... nor can he avoid what is unpleasant for him, such as bathwater so deep it frightens him, or constant pop music in the background

The person with more severe dementia will have difficulty initiating activities and interacting with others. He is unlikely to be able to help himself to even the simple pleasures of life, such as a walk in the garden or a favourite drink. In the same way he may be unable to avoid what is unpleasant for him, such as bathwater so deep it frightens him or constant pop-music in the background.

In more severe dementia, the whole quality of the person's life can depend entirely on the carer. If we fail to try to understand the unique needs of each person, we can seriously damage well-being.

The person with dementia has the right to lead as full and active a life as his illness will allow. However, it is vital that stimulation offered is appropriate both in terms of type of stimulation and amount.

WHY IS IT IMPORTANT THAT STIMULATION AND LEVELS OF ACTIVITY ARE APPROPRIATE?

A lack of appropriate stimulation can worsen the person's general health and mental status. It can lead to apathy and withdrawal. For the person with dementia who can not help himself to appropriate stimulation, it a bit like being in solitary confinement.

Too little stimulation or unsuitable stimulation

On the other hand, too much stimulation or unsuitable stimulation can lead to anxiety and panic.

Too much stimulation or unsuitable stimulation

Remember though that some people are happy to sit and watch what is going on around them for a while rather than be actively involved. The challenge is to learn to recognise if sitting and watching really is what the person wants at that time.

HOW DO I KNOW IF STIMULATION IS APPROPRIATE?

The carer needs to develop the skill of interpreting the person's non-verbal messages (see Chapter 12). Watching the person's facial expressions, eye contact and body language and listening to his emotional tone of voice may help you to learn what he does and does not enjoy.

Also of course, you need to think about the kind of activities the person may have enjoyed before his illness but bear in mind that interests can change. Activities must be tailored to individual needs and interests at any given time.

Remember also that the appropriate stimulation for an individual may be very basic – perhaps even as simple as holding someone's hand. Simple levels of stimulation such as using a soothing voice or a friendly smile can be incorporated creatively into daily care activities (see Chapter 12).

You may find it useful to record your impressions of the person's likes and dislikes in a structured way. The Cardiff Lifestyle Improvement Profile for People in Extended Residential Care (CLIPPER) has been designed with this in mind. Its aim is to help caregivers improve quality of life. Although the CLIPPER was designed to be used in a long-term care setting, it sometimes can be helpful for people in their own home.

The pilot version of the CLIPPER itself can be found in the appendices.

The CLIPPER considers 41 activities that could occur during a typical day. Caregivers note which activities occur, how often, and how the person seems to feel about each activity. This allows a care plan carefully to be tailored so as to create the best possible quality of life for each individual. Chapter 14 will describe the CLIPPER in more detail. For now, the 41 CLIPPER activities are listed below, along with a few suggestions for changes that could be considered. Glancing through the list highlights how dependent someone may become on caregivers for enriching quality of life.

TOUCH & MOVEMENT

Having a bath
- Is the water too hot?
- Is it too deep?
  - Sit more upright?
- Shower instead?
- Use bubble bath?
- Stop using bubble bath?
- Bath extra days in the week?
- Bath fewer days a week?
- Bath in the morning?
- Bath at night?
- Change person assisting with bathing (consider age/sex/culture etc.)?
- Use jacuzzi type jet stream?
- Use a hoist?
- Stop using a hoist?

Having a shower
- Bath instead of shower?
- Shower instead of bath?
- Would a shower seat help?
- Change pressure of water?
- Change height of shower head?

Having someone wash his/her hair
- Could hair be washed in a sink rather than in bath/shower?
- Use a special hair wash bowl for leaning backwards while sitting?
- Use a milder shampoo?
- Arrange visit to hairdresser?

Having someone comb/brush his/her hair
- Use a softer brush?
- Use mirror so person can see what is happening?
- Stop using a mirror?
- Change to style that requires less brushing/combing?
- Spend more time brushing/combing the person's hair?

Having someone cut his/her hair
- Change to a style that requires less frequent cutting?
- Involve person in choosing hair style (use pictures?).

Having someone clean his/her mouth
- Use a softer brush?
- Change flavour of toothpaste (eg to children's blackcurrant flavour)?
- Use electric toothbrush?

Having someone take care of his/her fingernails
- Make nail care a therapeutic activity?
- Cut nails rather than file nails?
- File nails rather than cut nails?
- Apply nail polish?
- Involve in choosing colour of nail polish?
- Stop using nail polish?

Having someone sit and hold his/her hand
- Encourage family to do this?
- Set special room aside for doing this?
- Stop doing this?

Having a hug
- Does he really like this?
- Is it happening enough?
- Encourage visitors not to feel embarrassed?
- Make private area available for visitors?

Having a hand/neck/foot/shoulder/body massage
- Incorporate hand cream into hand massage?
- Try electronic massager?
- Rocking chair?

Feeling and touching different objects, surfaces and textures
- Feelie items eg koosh ball, worry beads, stress ball, bendy tube?
- Feelie box with different objects and textures?

WATCHING & LISTENING

 Listening to music
- Purchase favourite tapes?
- Put together a tape of music that is personally significant?
- Use calming music (eg a tape of peaceful moods or Gregorian chant)?
- Music at bed time?
- Music while bathing?
- Stop playing certain music?
- Personal Walkman?

Listening to calming sounds (eg wind chimes, taped nature noises)
- Wind chime in personal area?
- Tape of natural sounds (eg nature sounds, sea sounds, whale song)?

 Looking at flowers/plants
- Favourite plants in personal area?
- Help to water and care for the plants?
- Visit florist/garden centre on a regular basis to choose potted plant for personal area?

 Looking at personal objects (eg soft toys, posters, ornaments)
- Obtain appropriate soft toy?
- Add relevant posters/ornaments to personal space?

Looking at special visual objects (eg mobiles, coloured glass etc.)
- Mobile eg coloured glass?
- Colourful sandglass?
- "Executive toys"?

TASTING & SMELLING

 Eating sweets, chocolates, etc.
- Visit local sweet shop regularly to choose confectionery? (But remember any special diets).

 Having special drinks (eg sherry, mineral water, Guinness etc.)
- Ask relatives to bring in bottle of sherry? (if the person can take alcohol).
- Encourage relatives/friends to share a drink with resident when visiting? (if the person can take alcohol).

Smelling "special smells" (eg air fresheners, perfume, aftershave)

- Use favourite perfume/aftershave?
- Take resident to choose new perfume?
- Obtain samples and let resident choose at home?
- Aroma diffuser?
- Incense?

PEOPLE & PETS

Having someone sit and talk to him/her

- Use memory album/"This is your life" album as focus for discussion? (See Chapter 5)
- Put memory album/"This is Your Life" story on audio or video tape?
- Help family (or person himself) to put memory album/"This is Your Life" story on audio or video tape?
- Encourage family/friends to make a taped "letter" for the person to listen to? The "letter" could talk about happy events from the distant past that the person may remember particularly well.
- Encourage "pairing up" with another resident?
- Try topics of personal and emotional importance that use "old memories"? (See Chapter 7.)

Having visitors

- Volunteer visitor?
- Encourage more visitors?
- Give visitors a purpose (eg involve in care or in activities)?

Watching or stroking pets

- Encourage family to bring in pets?
- "Pat-a-dog scheme"?
- Pet shaped cuddly toy with similar fur to familiar pet (eg smooth cat fur, rough dog hair)?

ACTIVITIES – ALONE OR ONE-TO-ONE

Watching the television

- Personal television at bedside?
- Very simple remote control?
- Highlight relevant programmes in TV magazine daily?
- Special interest videos (eg old home town, famous sports final, etc)?
- Non-verbal videos or videos which limit demands on memory and thinking (eg music with scenery, ice-skating, dog trials, wildlife – see chapter 8)?

Singing songs/hymns

- Song tapes to sing along to?
- Large print song sheets?
- Singing group?

Choosing which clothes to wear
- Encourage choice but simplify choices (eg offer choice of two outfits rather than 10)?

Looking at photos of self/family/friends
- Use memory album/"This is Your Life Album"? (See Chapter 5)
- Noticeboard in personal areas with family photos clearly labelled?
- Individual framed photos of family/friends with names clearly written on each (eg Janet, my daughter)?

Looking at "Special Interest" books (eg cars, home town, cats)
- Buy own selection of books?

Reading or browsing through books/magazines/newspapers
- Deliver personal newspaper/magazine daily or weekly?
- Give help with going through magazines/newspapers and encourage discussion?

Doing simple jigsaws
- Simple adult puzzles (eg 10-piece reminiscence puzzles)?

Doing simple handicrafts eg knitting, woodwork, etc.
- Printing?
- Sanding?
- Knitting squares for charity blankets?
- Rug making?
- Threading beads?

Helping with simple "household'" jobs eg dusting, making beds, etc.
- Regularly sort out cutlery drawer?
- Lay table?

ACTIVITIES – GROUPS

Attending an exercise group, eg exercise to music
- Continue exercise tape from group on an individual basis?
- Ask family to join in exercise tape while visiting?

Social groups eg discussion, reminiscence, gardening, cooking
- Encourage person to attend relevant group?
- Start up a small group with one or two other residents?

Playing group games or sports, eg skittles, bowls, snooker, etc.
- Encourage person to attend relevant group?
- Start up a small group with one or two other residents?
- Velcro darts?
- Ring board?

Playing table games or board games
- Bar skittles?
- Shove ha'penny?
- Bagatelle?
- Dominoes?

Attending a religious group or service
- Arrange for local clergy to visit?
- Attend service at local church?
- Visit local church at a non-service time?
- Talking bible?

ACTIVITIES – OUTDOORS

Going outside for a walk or being pushed outside in a wheelchair
- Link arms and walk outside?

Sitting outside in the fresh air when the weather is fine
- Sit outside with the person?
- Buy sunhat?
- Buy sunglasses?
- Buy garden umbrella?

ACTIVITIES – TRIPS, VISITS etc.

Going for a ride in a bus/car
- Encourage family/friends to take out?
- Take out with other residents?

Visiting family/friends at home
- Encourage family/friends to take home?

Going out to public places (eg theatre, shops, parks, museums)
- Plan regular trips out?
- Involve family and friends?

Many of the ideas above seem very simple. Yet the simple can become very special for people with dementia. Some may develop a great interest in very ordinary things, the sort of things that often we no longer notice in our busy lives – flowers, the clouds, the sky, an aeroplane.

It is well worth making the effort to enter into the person's world and think about changes that could make a real difference to their life.

14 Quality of life in more severe dementia: example of an individualised lifestyle profile

• How to use the CLIPPER to build up a unique profile of a person's likes and dislikes • Using the questionnaire and worksheet; planning and reviewing care

Chapter 13 looked at how important it is to make sure that the person with more severe dementia is helped towards achieving the best possible quality of life. To help achieve this, it can be helpful to use a formal individualised lifestyle profile.

The CLIPPER (Cardiff Lifestyle Improvement Profile for People in Extended Residential Care) allows caregivers to build up a unique profile of a person's likes and dislikes. This can help caregivers focus in on changes that could make a real difference.

The CLIPPER looks at how the person feels about 41 activities that could occur during the day. The activities are grouped into eight categories: TOUCH & MOVEMENT; WATCHING & LISTENING; TASTING & SMELLING; PEOPLE & PETS; ACTIVITIES – Alone or One-to-one; ACTIVITIES – Groups; ACTIVITIES – Outdoors; ACTIVITIES – Trips, Visits etc. Some activities are more passive while others encourage the person to be more actively involved.

The pilot version of the CLIPPER is in the appendices.

USING THE CLIPPER

Stage 1 – CLIPPER questionnaire (see figure 1 below).

The caregiver notes which of the 41 activities occur and how the person seems to feel about each activity. For example, to the question, *"Does the person now have a bath?"*, the caregiver should circle one of the following: YES and likes it; YES but dislikes it; YES but can't tell if he/she likes it or dislikes it; NO this never happens.

To answer the question, the caregiver will need to consider the person's verbal and non-verbal reactions (see Chapter 12). The opinions of other staff, family and friends should also be sought where appropriate. This will give an overall impression of well-being or displeasure when the person is having a bath.

Care to communicate

Stage 1: CLIPPER QUESTIONNAIRE

Name of Resident:

Date:

Completed by:

Indicate how you think the person feels about each activity.
Ask other staff, family and friends for their opinion where appropriate.

**The questions refer to the present time,
not how the person felt in the past.**

Does the person now **have a bath?**

| | YES and likes it | YES but dislikes it | YES but can't tell if he/she likes it or dislikes it | NO this never happens now |

Does the person now **have a shower?**

| | YES and likes it | YES but dislikes it | YES but can't tell if he/she likes it or dislikes it | NO this never happens now |

Does the person now **have someone wash his/her hair?**

| | YES and likes it | YES but dislikes it | YES but can't tell if he/she likes it or dislikes it | NO this never happens now |

Does the person now **have someone comb his/her hair?**

| | YES and likes it | YES but dislikes it | YES but can't tell if he/she likes it or dislikes it | NO this never happens now |

Does the person now **have someone cut his/her hair?**

| | YES and likes it | YES but dislikes it | YES but can't tell if he/she likes it or dislikes it | NO this never happens now |

Does the person now **have someone clean his/her mouth?**

| | YES and likes it | YES but dislikes it | YES but can't tell if he/she likes it or dislikes it | NO this never happens now |

Figure 1   *Stage 1 – The CLIPPER QUESTIONNAIRE (first page shown)*

USING THE CLIPPER

Stage 2 – CLIPPER worksheet (see figure 2, opposite).
Once the caregiver has answered the same question for all 41 activities, the answers are transferred to the CLIPPER WORKSHEET.

In the first column of the worksheet, activities that are liked are ticked. The second column documents activities that are disliked. The third column shows the can't tell activities, that is those activities for which it is impossible to tell how the individual feels. The fourth column shows activities that never happen.

When the worksheet is completed, it gives a visual summary or profile of the person's daily life.

The caregiver then thinks about possible changes that could be made to make life more enjoyable. Others involved in the person's care should be asked for their ideas too, including family and friends. Ideas for changes are noted on the worksheet.

CLIPPER WORKSHEET ACTIVITY	Things he/she LIKES	Can we make any of these even more enjoyable? Or do more often?	Things he/she DISLIKES	Can we change anything about any of these? Or do less often?	CAN'T TELL if likes or dislikes these things	Can we improve any of these to make them enjoyable?	Things that NEVER HAPPEN	Should we try any of these?
TOUCH & MOVEMENT								
Having a bath		☐		☐		☐		☐
Having a shower		☐		☐		☐		☐
Having someone wash his/her hair		☐		☐		☐		☐
Having someone comb/brush his/her hair		☐		☐		☐		☐
Having someone cut his/her hair		☐		☐		☐		☐
Having someone clean his/her mouth		☐		☐		☐		☐
Having someone take care of his/her fingernails		☐		☐		☐		☐
Having someone sit and hold his/her hand		☐		☐		☐		☐
Having a hug		☐		☐		☐		☐
Having a hand/neck/foot/shoulder/body massage		☐		☐		☐		☐
Feeling and touching different objects, surfaces and textures		☐		☐		☐		☐
WATCHING & LISTENING								
Listening to music		☐		☐		☐		☐
Listening to calming sounds eg windchimes, taped nature sounds		☐		☐		☐		☐
Looking at flowers/plants		☐		☐		☐		☐
Looking at personal objects eg soft toys, posters, ornaments		☐		☐		☐		☐
Looking at special visual objects eg mobiles, coloured glass, etc		☐		☐		☐		☐
TASTING & SMELLING								
Eating sweets, chocolates etc		☐		☐		☐		☐
Having special drinks eg sherry, mineral water, Guinness, etc		☐		☐		☐		☐
Smelling "special smells" eg air fresheners, perfume, aftershave		☐		☐		☐		☐
PEOPLE & PETS								
Having someone sit and talk to him/her		☐		☐		☐		☐
Having visitors		☐		☐		☐		☐
Watching or stroking pets		☐		☐		☐		☐
ACTIVITIES – Alone or one-to-one								
Watching the television		☐		☐		☐		☐
Singing songs/hymns		☐		☐		☐		☐
Choosing which clothes to wear		☐		☐		☐		☐
Looking at photos of self/family/friends		☐		☐		☐		☐
Looking at "special interest" books eg cars, home town, cats		☐		☐		☐		☐
Reading or browsing through books/magazines/newspapers		☐		☐		☐		☐
Doing simple jigsaws		☐		☐		☐		☐
Doing simple handicrafts eg knitting, woodwork, etc		☐		☐		☐		☐
Helping with simple "household" jobs eg dusting, making beds, etc		☐		☐		☐		☐
ACTIVITIES – Groups								
Attending an exercise group eg exercise to music		☐		☐		☐		☐
Social groups eg discussion, reminiscence, gardening, cooking		☐		☐		☐		☐
Playing group games or sports eg skittles, bowls, snooker, etc		☐		☐		☐		☐
Playing table or board games		☐		☐		☐		☐
Attending a religious group or service		☐		☐		☐		☐
ACTIVITIES – Outdoors								
Going outside for a walk or being pushed outside in a wheelchair		☐		☐		☐		☐
Sitting outside in the fresh air when the weather is fine		☐		☐		☐		☐
ACTIVITIES – Trips, visits, etc								
Going for a ride in a bus/car		☐		☐		☐		☐
Visiting family/friends at home		☐		☐		☐		☐
Going out to public places eg theatre, shops, parks, museums		☐		☐		☐		☐
	Other things he/she LIKES		Other things he/she DISLIKES					

Figure 2 *Stage 2: CLIPPER WORKSHEET. Information from the CLIPPER questionnaire is transferred to the worksheet. Suggestions for changes that could improve the person's lifestyle are then noted down.*

USING THE CLIPPER

Stage 3 – CLIPPER plan (see figure 3, opposite).

In Stage 3 of the CLIPPER programme, changes that are to be tried are recorded on a formal plan and a review date is set. Caregivers and family aim to try as many of the planned changes as possible before the review. The review is usually set for 1-3 months later.

Figure 3 shows how suggestions for changes for a gentleman called Mr. H. were entered onto the CLIPPER PLAN. The reasons why these particular changes were planned for Mr H are described below.

Mr H is a man who was noted to like looking at flowers and plants. The plan was:
• To help Mr H inspect the houseplants daily.
• To help Mr H water the plants regularly.
• To take Mr H to the garden centre by car every 2 weeks or so to choose and buy flowering plants.

He was noted to dislike having a bath. On discussion with his wife, staff thought that he may be embarrassed. The plan was
• To ask Mrs H to bath her husband once or twice a week.
It was felt that this would also help Mrs H who had only recently given up the total care of her husband.

Mr H did not seem to respond to music, although staff knew that he had previously been a keen musician. The plan was:
• To find out from Mr H's family what music he liked.
• To ask family to bring in tapes.
• To encourage Mr H to use his personal Walkman.

Mr H never looked at photos of self, family or friends and there were no photos present. The plan was:
• To help Mr H make a "THIS IS YOUR LIFE" memory album.
• To go through the album with Mr H several times a week.
• To ask Mr H's wife to bring photos in to be placed in his room.

Mr H was diabetic and never ate desserts despite the fact that his wife said this had previously been a great passion. The plan was:
• To check with a dietitian if a daily dessert could be incorporated into his diet and if so, to ask his wife to bring in desserts.
Again it was felt this would be a great help to Mrs H.

ACTIVITY ↓	**Stage 3: PLAN** Date of Plan: Changes to Try
LOOKING AT FLOWERS + PLANTS (LIKES)	(a) Help Mr H "inspect" houseplants daily (b) Help Mr H water the plants regularly (c) Car trip to garden centre every 2 weeks to buy flowering plant
BATHING (DISLIKES) ?embarrassed	(a) Ask wife if she will bath Mr H once or twice a week
LISTENING TO MUSIC (CAN'T TELL)	(a) Find out from family what music he used to like (b) Ask family to bring in tapes (c) Encourage Mr H to use personal walkman daily
LOOKING AT PHOTOS OF SELF/FAMILY/ FRIENDS (NEVER HAPPENS)	(a) Help make "This is Your Life" memory album (b) Go through album with Mr H several times a week (c) Photos around personal area
EATING SWEET DESSERTS (NEVER HAPPENS)	(a) Check with dietitian if can have daily dessert (b) Ask wife to bring in desserts

Figure 3 *Stage 3: CLIPPER PLAN. Suggestions for changes to be tried are entered on the plan. A review date is then set.*

USING THE CLIPPER

Stage 4 – CLIPPER review (see figure 4, opposite).
Stage 4 of the CLIPPER programme is the REVIEW. This looks at whether the changes seem to have improved the person's quality of life.

For each activity, the caregiver and others involved in the person's care answer the questions below:

Were the changes to this activity tried?
    YES; NO

Did the changes to the activity at any time improve his/her quality of life?
    YES; NO; Don't Know; None Tried.

Overall, are the changes to the activity improving his/her quality of life now?
    YES; NO; Don't Know; None Tried.

To answer these questions, carers will need to consider the person's verbal and non-verbal responses to the changes and the overall appearance of pleasure or displeasure as a result of the changes.

The whole cycle can then be repeated.

ACTIVITY	**Stage 3: PLAN** Date of Plan: Changes to Try	**Stage 4: REVIEW** Date of Review: Was this tried?	Did the changes to the activity at any time improve his/her quality of life?	Overall, are the changes to the activity improving his/her quality of life now?	Changes to add to new Plan
LOOKING AT FLOWERS + PLANTS (LIKES)		YES NO / YES NO / YES NO	YES NO / Don't Know None Tried	YES NO / Don't Know None Tried	
BATHING (DISLIKES) ?embarrassed		YES NO / YES NO / YES NO	YES NO / Don't Know None Tried	YES NO / Don't Know None Tried	
LISTENING TO MUSIC (CAN'T TELL)		YES NO / YES NO / YES NO	YES NO / Don't Know None Tried	YES NO / Don't Know None Tried	
LOOKING AT PHOTOS (NEVER HAPPENS)		YES NO / YES NO / YES NO	YES NO / Don't Know None Tried	YES NO / Don't Know None Tried	
EATING SWEET DESSERTS (NEVER		YES NO / YES NO / YES NO	YES NO / Don't Know None Tried	YES NO / Don't Know None Tried	
		YES NO / YES NO / YES NO	YES NO / Don't Know None Tried	YES NO / Don't Know None Tried	
		YES NO / YES NO / YES NO	YES NO / Don't Know None Tried	YES NO / Don't Know None Tried	
		YES NO / YES NO / YES NO	YES NO / Don't Know None Tried	YES NO / Don't Know None Tried	
		YES NO / YES NO / YES NO	YES NO / Don't Know None Tried	YES NO / Don't Know None Tried	
		YES NO / YES NO / YES NO	YES NO / Don't Know None Tried	YES NO / Don't Know None Tried	
		YES NO / YES NO / YES NO	YES NO / Don't Know None Tried	YES NO / Don't Know None Tried	

Planned date for review:

Figure 4   Stage 4: CLIPPER REVIEW. 1-3 months later the CLIPPER PLAN is reviewed to see which changes have taken place and the effects on quality of life.

The CLIPPER does not claim to be doing anything new. It is just a tool to help caregivers think about what is happening for an individual. This ensures that all possibilities for change are considered and that the best possible quality of life is achieved.

FINAL THOUGHTS...

Caring for the person with dementia involves working in partnership with the person themself, family and other caregivers to achieve the best possible quality of life. Each person's experience of dementia is unique. Not all the ideas in this book will work for everyone and different ideas are likely to be appropriate for different people at different times. Sometimes all that is needed is to "be there". Maintaining a creative and open mind, and seeing the world as the person with dementia sees it, will enable caregivers to offer the richest care possible. It can be a challenging but rewarding journey.

The year _____

MONDAY ___ ___	TUESDAY ___ ___	WEDNESDAY ___ ___	THURSDAY ___ ___	FRIDAY ___ ___	SATURDAY ___ ___	SUNDAY ___ ___

Name

I was born on _____ 19___

in

(Space for a photograph of yourself
as a baby or child if you have one.)

✂ -

My parents were

(Space for a photograph of your parents
if you have one. An early photograph if possible.)

During my childhood I lived ...

Schools I went to ...

✂ -

My brothers and sisters ...

_____ now living in

(Space for a photograph of yourself
when you were school age if you have one.)

(Space for a photograph of your brothers and sisters
as children if you have one.)

I left school when I was about _____ years old.
When I first left school I ...

(Space for a photograph of yourself as a young adult at around this time if you have one.)

✂

I worked until I was about _____ years of age.

Most of my working life I worked as ...

(Space for a photograph of yourself when you were at work, at your retirement or soon after retirement if you have one.)

The last job I had before retiring was ...

THIS IS MY LIFE

(Space for a photograph of yourself when you got married if you have one.)

My husband's name ...

We met ...

We were married on _____ 19___

at

My wife's name ...

We met ...

We were married on _____ 19___

at

When we were first married we lived in ...

Other places I have lived ...

My address now is ...

(Space for a photograph of you
at your present home.)

I had one child _____

who was born on _____ 19___

✂ -

I had _____ children...

_____ was born on _____ 19___

Holidays when the children were young ...

(Space for a photo of holidays when the children were young.)

(Space for a photo of the children when they were young.)

(Space for a photo of holidays when the children were young.)

My son _____ is married to _____.

They live in _____.

They have _____ children ...

_____ born in the year _____

My son _____ is married to _____.

They live in _____.

They have _____ children ...

_____ born in the year _____

My son _____ is married to _____.

They live in _____.

They have _____ children ...

_____ born in the year _____

My son _____ is married to _____.

They live in _____.

They have _____ children ...

_____ born in the year _____

My daughter _____ is married to _____.

They live in _____.

They have _____ children ...

_____ born in the year _____

My daughter _____ is married to _____.

They live in _____.

They have _____ children ...

_____ born in the year _____

My daughter _____ is married to _____.

They live in _____.

They have _____ children ...

_____ born in the year _____

My daughter _____ is married to _____.

They live in _____.

They have _____ children ...

_____ born in the year _____

(Space for a photograph of your son/daughter as they are now, perhaps with their husband/wife and children.)

(Space for a photograph of your son/daughter as they are now, perhaps with their husband/wife and children.)

(Space for a photograph of your son/daughter as they are now, perhaps with their husband/wife and children.)

(Space for a photograph of your son/daughter as they are now, perhaps with their husband/wife and children.)

Recent holidays ...

(Space for a photo of a recent holiday.)

Special friends and other important family members ...

(Space for a photo of a special friend or other important family member.)

Special pets past and present ...

(Space for a photo of a special pet.)

Important events ...

(Space for a photo of an important event.)

Stage 1: CLIPPER QUESTIONNAIRE

Name of Resident:

Date:

Completed by:

Indicate how you think the person feels about each activity.
Ask other staff, family and friends for their opinion where appropriate.

The questions refer to the present time,
not how the person felt in the past.

Does the person now **have a bath?**

	YES and likes it	YES but dislikes it	YES but can't tell if he/she likes it or dislikes it	NO this never happens now

---

Does the person now **have a shower?**

	YES and likes it	YES but dislikes it	YES but can't tell if he/she likes it or dislikes it	NO this never happens now

---

Does the person now **have someone wash his/her hair?**

	YES and likes it	YES but dislikes it	YES but can't tell if he/she likes it or dislikes it	NO this never happens now

---

Does the person now **have someone comb his/her hair?**

	YES and likes it	YES but dislikes it	YES but can't tell if he/she likes it or dislikes it	NO this never happens now

---

Does the person now **have someone cut his/her hair?**

	YES and likes it	YES but dislikes it	YES but can't tell if he/she likes it or dislikes it	NO this never happens now

---

Does the person now **have someone clean his/her mouth?**

	YES and likes it	YES but dislikes it	YES but can't tell if he/she likes it or dislikes it	NO this never happens now

---

Does the person now **eat sweets or chocolates?**

YES and likes it	YES but dislikes it	YES but can't tell if he/she likes it or dislikes it	NO this never happens now

Does the person now **have special drinks, eg sherry, mineral water, Guinness etc?**

YES and likes it	YES but dislikes it	YES but can't tell if he/she likes it or dislikes it	NO this never happens now

Does the person now **smell "special smells", eg air fresheners, perfume, aftershave?**

YES and likes it	YES but dislikes it	YES but can't tell if he/she likes it or dislikes it	NO this never happens now

Does the person now **have someone sit and talk to him/her?**

YES and likes it	YES but dislikes it	YES but can't tell if he/she likes it or dislikes it	NO this never happens now

Does the person now **have visitors?**

YES and likes it	YES but dislikes it	YES but can't tell if he/she likes it or dislikes it	NO this never happens now

Does the person now **watch or stroke pets?**

YES and likes it	YES but dislikes it	YES but can't tell if he/she likes it or dislikes it	NO this never happens now

Does the person now **watch the television?**

YES and likes it	YES but dislikes it	YES but can't tell if he/she likes it or dislikes it	NO this never happens now

Does the person now **sing songs/hymns?**

YES and likes it	YES but dislikes it	YES but can't tell if he/she likes it or dislikes it	NO this never happens now

Does the person now **choose which clothes to wear?**

YES and likes it	YES but dislikes it	YES but can't tell if he/she likes it or dislikes it	NO this never happens now

Does the person now **look at photos of self/family/friends?**

YES and likes it	YES but dislikes it	YES but can't tell if he/she likes it or dislikes it	NO this never happens now

Does the person now **look at special interest books, eg cars, home town, cats?**

| YES and likes it | YES but dislikes it | YES but can't tell if he/she likes it or dislikes it | NO this never happens now |

Does the person now **read or browse through books/magazines/newspapers?**

| YES and likes it | YES but dislikes it | YES but can't tell if he/she likes it or dislikes it | NO this never happens now |

Does the person now **do simple jigsaws?**

| YES and likes it | YES but dislikes it | YES but can't tell if he/she likes it or dislikes it | NO this never happens now |

Does the person now **do simple handicrafts, eg knitting, woodwork, etc?**

| YES and likes it | YES but dislikes it | YES but can't tell if he/she likes it or dislikes it | NO this never happens now |

Does the person now **help with simple "household" jobs, eg dusting, making beds, etc?**

| YES and likes it | YES but dislikes it | YES but can't tell if he/she likes it or dislikes it | NO this never happens now |

Does the person now **attend an exercise group, eg exercise to music?**

| YES and likes it | YES but dislikes it | YES but can't tell if he/she likes it or dislikes it | NO this never happens now |

Does the person now **attend "social groups", eg discussion group, reminiscence group, gardening group, cooking group?**

| YES and likes it | YES but dislikes it | YES but can't tell if he/she likes it or dislikes it | NO this never happens now |

Does the person now **play group games or sports, eg skittles, bowls, snooker, etc?**

| YES and likes it | YES but dislikes it | YES but can't tell if he/she likes it or dislikes it | NO this never happens now |

Does the person now **play table or board games?**

| YES and likes it | YES but dislikes it | YES but can't tell if he/she likes it or dislikes it | NO this never happens now |

Does the person now **attend a religious group or service?**

| YES and likes it | YES but dislikes it | YES but can't tell if he/she likes it or dislikes it | NO this never happens now |

Does the person now **go outside for a walk (or is pushed outside in a wheelchair?)**

| YES and likes it | YES but dislikes it | YES but can't tell if he/she likes it or dislikes it | NO this never happens now |

Does the person now **sit outside in the fresh air when the weather is fine?**

| YES and likes it | YES but dislikes it | YES but can't tell if he/she likes it or dislikes it | NO this never happens now |

Does the person now **go for a ride in a bus/car?**

| YES and likes it | YES but dislikes it | YES but can't tell if he/she likes it or dislikes it | NO this never happens now |

Does the person now **visit family/friends at their home?**

| YES and likes it | YES but dislikes it | YES but can't tell if he/she likes it or dislikes it | NO this never happens now |

Does the person now **go out to public places, eg theatre, shops, parks, museums?**

| YES and likes it | YES but dislikes it | YES but can't tell if he/she likes it or dislikes it | NO this never happens now |

Other activities the person seems to **like** now:

Other activities the person seems to **dislike** now:

The information on this CLIPPER QUESTIONNAIRE should be transferred to the CLIPPER WORKSHEET (Stage 2)

CLIPPER

Cardiff Lifestyle Improvement Profile for People in Extended Residential care

Stage 2: CLIPPER WORKSHEET

Instructions

* Transfer the information from the CLIPPER QUESTIONNAIRE to the CLIPPER WORKSHEET to give a visual profile of the resident's lifestyle.

* Then use the WORKSHEET to identify changes that could be tried in order to improve the resident's lifestyle. Write your suggestions on the WORKSHEET.

For activities the person dislikes:
Think about why the person may dislike the activity and try to change those things about the activity. Is there a different way of doing it? Does it need to be done at all?

For activities the person likes:
Can the activity be changed to make it even more enjoyable? Should it happen more often? Be very specific, eg "go for a short walk around the grounds at least three times a week" not "walk more often".

For activities that never happen:
Should any of these activities be tried? Be very specific about how the activity will be tried – eg who will be involved, when, who needs to be contacted, etc.

For activities when you can't tell if it is liked or disliked:
Can the activity be changed in any way to make it enjoyable? Be very specific.

PLEASE NOTE:
Not all of the 41 CLIPPER activities will be appropriate for everyone. If you have any doubts about the suitability of an activity, check with the relevant professional. Any actions taken or changes made should take into account the individual's mental and physical state and the overall clinical situation.

Name:

Worksheet Number:

Date of Worksheet:

Primary Worker:

Home Manager/Other Facilitator:

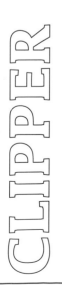

CLIPPER

Cardiff Lifestyle Improvement Profile for People in Extended Residential care

Stage 3: CLIPPER PLAN

Date of Plan:

Plan based on Worksheet Number:

Instructions

* Transfer the changes suggested on the CLIPPER WORKSHEET to the inside of this PLAN.

* Set a date for REVIEW of the planned changes (usually 4 to 6 weeks but could be sooner or up to 3 months as appropriate).

* Inform others involved in resident's care of changes that are to be tried.

* Leave PLAN where it can be accessed easily on a day-to-day basis.

Stage 4: CLIPPER REVIEW

Date of Review:

Instructions

* For each activity for which changes were planned, answer the questions on the inside of this sheet under the heading REVIEW.

Name:

Primary Worker:

Home Manager/Other Facilitator: